SOUTHERN WAY

Spe

SOUTHERN COLOUR IN THE SIXTIES

a second selection

Terry Cole

NOODLE BOOKS

ISBN   978-1-906419-56-1

First published in 2011 by Kevin Robertson
under the **NOODLE BOOKS** imprint
PO Box 279
Corhampton
SOUTHAMPTON
SO32 3ZX

www.noodlebooks.co.uk.

Printed in England by Ian Allan Printing

Front Cover: The Pulborough – Midhurst line, September 1963. Q1 class 33018 waits at Petworth with the twice weekly goods train. The limited number of wagons being hauled illustrates the reduced nature of the freight operation at the time; the passenger service had ceased years before. The autumnal tints and the fading paintwork of the station building do rather echo the state of the line.

Frontispiece: Semaphore signals and manual signalboxes at frequent intervals along the line were a feature of railways from the earliest days. Today the vast majority have been replaced by new remote control centres covering large stretches of the network. Here, at Christ's Hospital, we see the signalbox which controlled the junction of the Guildford branch. In the centre is the up mainline starting signal on a typical Southern Railway rail-built post. (Authors collection)

Opposite: Summer 1965. O2 class W14 'Fishbourne' crosses Newport viaduct on the Isle of Wight with a passenger train heading for Cowes.

Back Cover: Petworth station and yard from the road overbridge. Q1 class 33018 is waiting to return to Pulborough with just a few wagons in September 1963.

All the photographs included were taken by the author with the exception of those he has collected from various sources and which are credited to his personal collection or those of others.

PREFACE

It was quite by chance that I took my first railway photograph in 1954. Bulleid Electric locomotive 20001 had stopped at the signal outside the house where I lived in West Worthing. This was an unusual event: clearly something had gone wrong further up the line. I rushed indoors, grabbed my 'Brownie 127' and took my snap. Soon I was photographing more locomotives: Ks, C2Xs, E4s, West Countries and Atlantics not to mention the newly built Standard 4 Tanks then being out-shopped from Brighton Works. Publications like Trains Illustrated introduced me to what railway photography was all about and soon my interest widened to include not just the locomotives but the trains they were hauling. As I mentioned in my previous book, cost prevented me from taking colour until 1963 when a Saturday job stacking shelves in the local supermarket was putting a bit more money in my pocket. The shock of the mass withdrawals of the locomotives I had grown to know and which I had fully expected to continue on the railway scene, prompted me to take some colour photographs, more of an extra than a replacement for black and white. So I took a roll of colour at Eastleigh in March 1963. It wasn't until I had taken a second roll several months later on the Exe Valley and Hemyock branches in Devon that I fully realised what I was missing. From now on it had to be colour! Time was fast running out. In fact I didn't realise how little was left. But somehow by bike, train or in my antique van I did manage to get to local lines before they closed and before steam disappeared. With hindsight I wish I had done more but I did not foresee the speed of events. As a rule I favoured country branch lines and wayside stations in an attempt to capture what I was aiming for: steam in the landscape.

This second selection is again a very personal one. I have tried to recreate my own days of train spotting and photography rather than provide a comprehensive overview. There is less focus on my immediate home area but my choices still centre on West Sussex and surrounding counties, the places most accessible to me. Again the photographs are grouped in chapters, each covering a different line.

All of these pictures were taken 40 years ago and one of or two may not meet the standards of today's digital technology. Nevertheless I trust that readers will appreciate their value as archive material and be willing to overlook any technical shortcomings.

I hope that this collection will be of interest to those who wish to indulge in pure nostalgia as well as to modellers and railway historians.

Terry Cole

Steyning, May 2011

CONTENTS

Introduction

Nowadays it is difficult to imagine the crucial role played by the railways in the first half of the twentieth century. Whatever had to be moved: passengers, livestock, coal, freight of all kinds, there was only one practicable means of transport. What is more, as 'common carriers' the railways were obliged to accept whatever was brought to them and to take it wherever directed. This is amply illustrated in the great ledgers with their tables of charges for the transport of everything from a parrot to a pushchair, anywhere from Inverness to Penzance, held at every station in the land. At this point in time the railway along with the church, the village stores and the pub occupied a central place in the life of the community.

However the context was to change. By the end of the Second World War the four major companies were virtually bankrupt. If they were to survive and prosper, nationalisation offered the only solution and indeed this became a reality on 1st January 1948.

Initially little changed. Orders for locomotives already placed continued to be delivered throughout the first half of the 1950s. It was a fact that the nationalised railways had inherited a large selection of antique and in many cases life-expired locomotives. In order to speed up modernisation, the newly established British Railways introduced 'Standard' designs incorporating best practice from the original companies to cover the range of duties now required. No. 70000 'Britannia', which appeared in January1951, was the first of these new locomotives. By the time No. 92220 'Evening Star' emerged from Swindon Works in March 1960, a total of 999 had been built. So by the mid 1950s British Railways had a large and growing fleet of modern steam locomotives with rolling stock to match.

Then the game changed. A second modernisation plan determined that electrification and diesel power alone represented the way ahead and that steam should be replaced as quickly as possible. However this was not all. In political circles there grew a belief that the railways themselves constituted an outdated mode of transport and that the car and the lorry held the keys to the future. As always, politics determines the rise and fall of national institutions. Much was sacrificed in the headlong dash for new technology. The destruction that would follow was not appreciated, nor its wider consequences. The transport structures of the country were profoundly altered with no recognition or understanding of the total impact. Indeed it would not be unreasonable to compare the subsequent upheaval that occurred in the 10 years between 1955 and 1965 as a result of the dismantling of the railway network to the impact on society at large caused over the ten years between 2000 and 2010 by the arrival and growing influence of the Internet.

In the context of the railway network of the mid to late twentieth century, change was undoubtedly required. However the new philosophy was pushed through to the exclusion of all other considerations. In concrete terms resources were wasted on a vast scale. Some of the 'modern' locomotives lasted less than five years and very many less than ten, whereas older ones, retired at the same time, had served for 70 years. Lines were closed, land was sold off, often for derisory sums, thus reducing the scope for future development should priorities change. On occasions the 'economic argument' was applied or even misapplied specifically to secure permission for closures, regardless of other factors. Withdrawals of steam locomotives accelerated throughout the late 50s and early 60s, culminating on the Southern Region, with the decision to withdraw a large proportion of those remaining at the stroke of a pen. This occurred on December 31st 1962. Even so, steam did survive in the south longer than in some other regions. On the Isle of Wight for example, the 70 year old O2 class locomotives reigned supreme until December 1966, and the Waterloo to Bournemouth line had the distinction of being Britain's last steam operated mainline, until in July 1967 this was brought to an end by electrification.

The general picture is echoed in the fate of the individual lines featured in this publication. On the Southern as elsewhere motives for change varied as did the effects. The Pulborough to Midhurst branch had always been primarily sustained by freight with passenger traffic an uneconomic add-on. Indeed it became a freight only operation in 1955. So when the need to transport agricultural produce collapsed, the line was no longer viable and closure became inevitable. By contrast, passengers could have been the mainstay between East Grinstead and Three Bridges where feeder services for the Brighton to London main line were needed in the context of local housing development and working patterns. The Horsham to Guildford line was admittedly more problematic: the western half certainly had commuter potential and Surrey County Council wanted to keep it open, whereas their West Sussex counterparts were less than enthusiastic. Unfortunately the service operated at that time did nothing to encourage usage.

On the Isle of Wight, electrification of the route to Shanklin was an undoubted success whereas failure to electrify the Cowes line illustrates a missed opportunity. It was only on the South Western main line that steam was allowed to run its course until electrification took over.

One is led to conclude that the implementation of a single strategy with its over simplistic assessment failed many then, just as it does now: a situation best summed up by paraphrasing the Little Richard sixties song: "they got what they wanted even though they lost what they had."

Hove Goods Yard, 7th June 1963. Only a few of the locomotives that were dumped here at the start of the year remain. The majority of them have already been towed away for scrap. Featured here are three of those left: 'Schools' class No. 30923 'Bradfield', E6 class No. 32417, which spent its last days as shed pilot at Brighton, and an unidentified member of the U1 class. They await their last journeys.

(author's collection)

CHAPTER 1

Eastleigh Shed: early 1963

The winter of 1962/3 will be remembered for two reasons. Firstly it was very cold with snow lying on the ground for several weeks. Trains in the North of England were abandoned in snow drifts and towns and villages cut off. Here in the south the electric trains struggled through with much arcing as a result of ice on the conductor rails. Secondly it was the winter of the great cull of 'southern' steam locomotives, with virtually every pre 1923 locomotive, and a good many Southern Railway ones also, condemned on 31 December 1962. On my regular journeys travelling from Worthing to London and back I had seen the forlorn lines of discarded locomotives dumped in Hove Goods Yard. Word had it that a great many others had received the same treatment at Eastleigh. So in early March, when the snow had subsided, I travelled to Eastleigh to take a look and record some of them before they were consigned for scrap. The shed was indeed packed; every siding stuffed full of engines; the old and the new lined up side by side. Eastleigh had always been a train spotter's paradise. Today all was uniformly grey, the weather echoing the melancholy. A depressing scene: grimy engines, not a glimmer of light.

Above - The first picture I took on this occasion was of ex LSWR '700' class No. 30316, built in 1897, which I had seen around Eastleigh many times previously. Although officially withdrawn at the end of December, it had been fitted with a snow plough and had a few more outings in January and February. Now even those duties were over, but it would be some time before it was sent to the nearby Works for breaking up.

Opposite top - Class U1 31892 was built in 1931 at Eastleigh Works, one of 21 three-cylinder 2-6-0s. Used on both passenger and freight work No. 31892 finished its days at Three Bridges shed.

Opposite bottom - All the eight members of the 'Z' class were withdrawn en bloc at the end of 1962. Built at Brighton Works in 1929, they were extremely useful as heavy shunters and latterly as banking engines at Exeter. Here No. 30952 awaits the call to the Works for breaking up.

Opposite top - One of the oldest locomotives present was Adams 'O2' class No. 30225 built in 1892. It and No. 30199, also present that day, were the last two mainland survivors of the class. Both had been withdrawn at the end of December. The Isle of Wight version of the class however would continue to give stalwart service for another four years. (They can be seen at work in Chapter 5.)

Opposite lower - Urie S15 No. 30496 built for the LSWR in 1921. With the introduction of diesels on many of the area's freight services, redundancy loomed for this class of engine. The older locomotives were withdrawn; the more modern ones, designed by Maunsell, retained. No. 30496 was not officially withdrawn until June 1963 so at this point in March 1963 its operational status was unclear, although the twisted buffer beam may mean it would never work again.

Above - No. 30517 was one of five Urie designed express goods engines built in 1921. The other four had been withdrawn in November but No. 30517 had been active until Christmas. Here it is flanked by ex GWR Pannier Tank No. 4656 and Standard Class 4 Tank No. 80144. The Pannier Tank may have been transferred to the Southern to work at Folkestone Harbour or alternatively at Clapham Junction. However its stay was short lived because by December 1962 it had already been withdrawn. No. 80144 by contrast was returned to the Central section where it was active on the 'Cuckoo line'. It then went to Salisbury and thereafter to Nine Elms. It was from this shed that it was finally withdrawn from service in May 1966.

Above - In the back road, traditionally the repository of withdrawn engines, K class No. 32349, designed by Billinton for the LBSCR in 1913 awaits its fate. The coupling rods on this side have been removed together with the cylinder covers, indicating that something had gone wrong while it was being towed here. I must admit that I was devastated when the Ks were all withdrawn in late 1962. They were amongst my favourite engines. Not only had they worked right up until Christmas but some had recently been overhauled. It seemed such a waste!

Opposite top - An unusual locomotive. M7 No. 30378 was built in 1903 for the LSWR, one of ten long framed engines with their sandboxes inside the smokebox rather than combined with the front splashers. Its subsequent adaptation in February 1962 resulted in the engine we see here. There were originally four types of M7: those with long frames, others with short frames, some with combined sandbox-splashers, some without. It was the long framed version with combined sandbox-splashers that were used for push-pull conversion. Many of the other types had been withdrawn because diesels had taken over their work. However when the push-pull engines, which were still much in demand, wore out, there were no longer any suitable candidates for conversion. Options were limited because the short frame engines had insufficient room under the front buffer beam for installation of the air cylinder needed for the push-pull gear. Only those locomotives with separate sandboxes would allow for this. The result was the conversion of two of the remaining long-frame separate sandbox locomotives. However, 30378 only lasted in this form from February to December 1962.

Opposite lower - G16 No. 30494 was one of four 4-8-0 tank engines built by the LSWR in 1921 for hump shunting at Feltham yard and for heavy goods work. Both Nos. 30492 and 30493 had been withdrawn in 1959 when extensive repairs became necessary but Nos. 30494 and 30495 both survived until the end of 1962.

.

East Grinstead was a busy junction operating on two levels with lines radiating to each of the four points of the compass. The double track Low Level line headed south towards Horsted Keynes, Haywards Heath and Lewes and northwards towards Oxted and London. The High Level station crossed at right angles with single track lines running east towards Groombridge and Tunbridge Wells and west to Three Bridges. The station layout also incorporated a west bound link from the High Level that swung round to join the Low Level London line at St Margaret's Junction, a short distance to the north. The extensive goods yard occupied the land between the eastward and southern lines. The latter had closed in 1955 but reopened in 1956, only to close again in 1958. From 1955 onwards the Low Level station was little used although it did retain the station offices. The High Level remained fully operational but by 1963 Diesel Multiple Units had taken over much of the work. Some push-pull steam trains were still used to supplement the services in the rush hour. These were operated by the last remaining H or M7 tank engines based at Three Bridges shed.

Above - M7 No. 30053 pictured just east of East Grinstead High Level station in September 1963 with a push-pull train comprising two recently converted Maunsell coaches. These had been rebuilt between mid 1959 and early 1961.This version was short lived: rapidly phased out as a result of line closures or dieselisation. The last sets were withdrawn in November 1964. Although the train appears to be on double track that is not the case.

Opposite top - The same train as in the previous photograph. It is clear here that it is in fact waiting in a siding alongside the single line for its next turn of duty. Ironically the old track bed is now called Beeching Way, part of the East Grinstead relief road.

Opposite bottom - British Railways Standard class 4 No. 80085 at East Grinstead High Level in September 1964 carrying a 75B Redhill shedplate. It survived until the end of steam on the Southern in July 1967.

Previous page - 'East Sussex' Diesel Multiple Unit No. 1306 is entering East Grinstead High Level station from the direction of Three Bridges in September 1964. The signalman is collecting the single line train staff for the section from Grange Road. Curving away towards the right is the previously mentioned connection to the London line. Also featured are the lower quadrant signals on a concrete post. Few had survived to this time.

Above - M7 No. 30053 seen from East Grinstead Low Level station. At this time the Low Level was little used. However with the closure of the lines to Three Bridges and Groombridge in January 1967 the situation changed. This time the High Level was abandoned and London trains reverted to the Low Level, a situation which continues to the present day although the station is barely recognisable. When the Bluebell Railway Extension, currently under construction, is complete trains will once more run into East Grinstead from the south although they will terminate a short distance from the original station.

Opposite top - The same engine, No. 30053 and its push-pull train enter Grange Road station, past the tiny goods yard and loading dock. The crew are hanging out of the cab seemingly eager to have their photograph taken.

Opposite bottom - Grange Road station looking from the east. DEMU No. 1319 is waiting at the single platform before resuming its journey to East Grinstead. The attractive LBSCR signalbox can be seen on the right and the wonderful oil lamp that illuminated the exit from the station.

Previous page - M7 No. 30053 with its push-pull train leaving Grange Road for Rowfant and Three Bridges in September 1963. No. 30053, built for the London and South Western Railway in December 1905, was one of the last survivors. Withdrawn in May 1964, it was steamed again in June of that year before its sale for preservation in the United States. Since then it has returned to this country and is based on the Swanage Railway.

Above - Rowfant station with its two platforms, viewed from the level crossing. The main building was on the north side, with a shelter opposite. The white edges to the doorway brickwork are a survivor from the blackout of the Second World War.

Opposite top - No. 30053 leaving Rowfant, pushing its train back to East Grinstead. Only the fireman is on the footplate, the driver will be in his compartment at the front. Nobody seems bothered that the headcode disc has been left in place.

Opposite bottom - An unidentified BRCW Type 3 diesel seen at Rowfant signal box. The single line train staff has been collected by the crew from the signalman. Now the light engine can proceed.

Opposite top - H class No. 31263 pictured here, was probably working through from Tunbridge Wells with one of the rush hour extras, sharing duties on that afternoon with M7 No. 30053. Here the signalman exchanges a few words with the crew as they swap single line train staffs. The light is fading; always a problem when photographing late afternoon trains other than in summer.

Opposite bottom - Earlier that afternoon DEMU No. 1319 leaves Rowfant for Three Bridges. The width of the crossing can be appreciated together with the unusual location of the mile and gradient posts.

Above - September 1963: 'Just a glimpse then gone forever'. From an overbridge it was possible to capture a fleeting image of an M7 (probably No. 30053) pushing its train towards East Grinstead. Regular steam working ceased at the end of that year and Three Bridges shed closed.

Even DMU operation couldn't save the line. It closed on 2 January 1967. Today little remains.

CHAPTER 3
HORSHAM - GUILDFORD

WAY OUT

CHRIST'S HOSPITAL

WAY OUT
AND
PLATFORMS 1, 2 & 3

A

The Horsham to Guildford branch diverged from the ex LBSCR mainline at Christ's Hospital and ran through rural North Sussex and South Surrey to join the ex LSWR 'Portsmouth Direct' line at Peasmarsh Junction, just south of Guildford. It was single track throughout and restrictions on it prohibited the use of locomotives bigger than 0-6-0s. It could have been a useful through route to the south coast were it not for these restrictions and the fact that trains would have had to reverse at Horsham. There was a plan to build a triangular junction at Christ's Hospital but it was never implemented. The service was infrequent with just a few trains in morning and evening peak hours and the odd one or two during the day. Incidentally this also made it less attractive for photographers, at least so long as other lines had more frequent steam services. As far as I am aware Diesel Multiple Units never operated here.

Previous page - Christ's Hospital, April 1965. A train formed of a Bulleid 3-coach set and a van, headed by an ex LMS 2-6-2 tank crosses the junction in order to reach the Guildford line platforms. Passengers could move between the mainline platforms, 1 to 3, by means of a subway, but those arriving from Guildford on platform 5 had to cross over the Guildford tracks near the signal box to reach the main station.

Above - LMS designed 2-6-2 tank No. 41299 waits at Christ's Hospital in early June 1965 with a Guildford bound train. Boys from the nearby public school in their distinctive uniform can be seen on the platform. In fact this station was built to serve the school. It featured no fewer than five tracks, seven platform faces and magnificent buildings with ornamental brickwork.

Opposite top - Early June 1965. No. 41299 is about to depart from platform 5 at Christ's Hospital for Horsham. An explanation of the previously mentioned five tracks and seven platforms is perhaps due. In point of fact at this station it was the tracks that were numbered rather than the platforms. So two platforms carried the number 1 as both ran alongside single track No. 1. The same was true of track 4, seen below, with its two platforms. Tracks 2, 3 and 5 had just one platform each.

Opposite bottom - 2-6-2 tank No. 41301 is seen in April 1965 waiting at platform 4 with a Guildford bound train. Some of the ornamental brickwork can be glimpsed on the right but the mainline station buildings were much grander. Sadly they were demolished in the 1970s. All that was left were two bare platforms, numbers 2 and 3. Today it is little more than a halt, totally unrecognisable in contrast to the splendour of earlier times.

Opposite top - Christ's Hospital again, early June 1965. No. 41299 is waiting for the signal to depart for Guildford. The fact that the line was due to close on the 14th June was undoubtedly the reason for the interest shown in the locomotive and coaches by those on the platform. I wonder if the boy watching still remembers this scene from over 45 years ago.

Opposite bottom - A general view of the Guildford line platforms in April 1965. Near the signal box you can just make out the tall starting signal for the up mainline. Curiously the ground frame had to be operated each time a Guildford bound train left the station.

Above - The first station on the line was Slinfold. Here No. 41299 is waiting to depart for Horsham with 3-coach Bulleid set 865. The small ventilators at the top of the windows tell us that this is a genuine Southern Railway built coach rather than one of the more numerous ones from British Railways days. The latter had deep ventilators. In earlier days this line would have been operated by vintage push-pull trains but these had been withdrawn five years earlier.

Slinfold station basks in the afternoon spring sunshine in 1964. This neat little single track station served the nearby village.

On the same day
2-6-2 tank No. 41294
arrives at Slinfold with
an afternoon train from
Horsham.
The deterioration in the
care of the locomotives is
noticeable when this
clean engine is
compared with those
photographed the
following year. In the
foreground the ex
LBSCR wooden signal
post has had a
replacement Southern
Railway upper quadrant
arm fitted.

Above - No. 41299 pulls away from Slinfold en route to Horsham in early spring 1965.

Opposite top - A view from the bridge at the east end of Rudgwick station, taken in June 1964, shows the original LBSCR signal box and the tiny goods yard that had already fallen into disuse. The goods yard and box were at the Horsham end of the station whereas at Slinfold they were at the Guildford end. Without run round loops this must have made operating difficult. It is curious in that the goods headshunt ran straight on whereas the running line deviated to the right. A shot from this angle appeared on Formoway 'OO' point boxes in the 1960s.

Bottom right - June 1965, a view taken from a Horsham bound train of Baynards station. This boasted a totally different design. With two platforms it was an altogether bigger affair. The station gardens were magnificent in late summer with the station master's collection of prize dahlias in full bloom.

Above *-* By far the most important stop on the line was Cranleigh with its station at the heart of the small town. A 41xxx tank on its way to Guildford approaches Cranleigh in summer 1964. The station master has extended his garden on both sides of the line, rose bushes to the left, greenhouse and vegetable patch to the right. Many country stations were enlivened by flourishing gardens but few could compete with those at Baynards or Cranleigh.

Opposite top right - Cranleigh, seen from the footbridge looking towards Horsham. A few trains from Guildford terminated at Cranleigh, hence the 'Shunt ahead' signal located beneath the starting signal on the platform. This allowed the locomotive to draw forward within station limits and to run round its train without the signalman having to 'draw a train staff' for the next section of line.

Opposite bottom *-* A photograph taken from the window of a Horsham bound train in early June 1965 as it enters Cranleigh. A second train is waiting for it to clear the single line.

Next page - A general view of Cranleigh in June 1965 showing the signal box and main station buildings. Closure was only a few days away. The passengers on the platform, like me, were probably taking their last ride. Hence their interest in what is going on. Today all traces of the station have vanished and the site is occupied by a parade of shops.

Above – I didn't take any photographs of the last station, Bramley and Wonersh so we have now arrived at Guildford where No. 41296 is waiting to leave for Horsham.

Opposite top - Another view of Guildford this time with No. 41299. The leading coach is one of the original Bulleid vehicles built for the Bournemouth line with shallow ventilators and side sheeting extending below the footboards.

Opposite bottom - A view looking south from the overbridge at Guildford station with the 'roundhouse' hemmed in between the cliffs, the roadbridge and the tracks. The site of the shed is occupied now by a multi-storey car park. In the foreground Q class No. 30541. This locomotive survives today at the Bluebell Railway.

In the mid 1960s when the closure of the line was proposed local authorities had the opportunity to object. For its part Surrey County Council wanted to keep the Horsham- Guildford line open. They were prepared to subsidise it as the section from Cranleigh was quite busy in the rush hour. However West Sussex County Council were not prepared to contribute anything for the section within their boundaries. Because the route would only have been viable in its entirety and because no agreement was secured, it closed on 14th June 1965. Of the line itself little remains, just the odd footpath or unexpected road bridge to remind the traveller of its existence.

CHAPTER 4

PULBOROUGH – MIDHURST

To my mind the line from Pulborough to Midhurst ran through some of the most beautiful countryside in Sussex, if not in the whole of the South of England. Leaving the ex LBSCR mainline at Hardham Junction, one mile south of Pulborough, it followed the course of the River Rother. With the Downs to the south in the distance and the Sussex Weald spread out on either side, it ran through farmland dotted with old cottages, ancient oak woods and the occasional small village or market town. At Midhurst the line met end on with the ex LSWR branch from Petersfield. But it was only in the latter days of the Southern Railway that a through passenger service started to operate linking both parts. There was also a branch to Chichester, but the passenger service on it was withdrawn in the 1930s. All passenger services ceased in 1955. Goods traffic continued until the mid 1960s.

Previous page - Fittleworth was the first stop on the line. The pretty little station is photographed here from the road overbridge, looking towards Petworth, in October 1963. Although this station had closed to passengers 8 years earlier it was still intact. The tiny goods yard lay beyond the station. There was no signal box so the points would be unlocked by a 'key' on the end of the train staff. The yard could only be shunted by trains travelling in the Midhurst direction because there was no run round loop. This meant that traffic in the opposite direction had to make a long detour via Midhurst in order to reach Pulborough.

Above - Petworth, the second station on the line, seen here in 1963 basking in the sunshine of a September morning. The wooden station building is decorated with diagonal planking at top and foot of its walls, an unusual feature.

Opposite top - Petworth again in September 1963. No. 33018 is shown waiting with the twice weekly pick up goods service. In fact Petworth was the principal intermediate station on the line. It had a large yard, a goods shed, a passing loop and a signal box. However the fact that the station had to be built out in the country a good two miles south of the thriving market town it was designed to serve, effectively dashed all hopes of sustainable passenger traffic. This location was the result of landowner pressure from nearby Petworth House.

Opposite bottom - A view of Petworth looking towards Pulborough shows the signalbox, goods shed and site of the former passing loop. Just visible are coal wagons being unloaded in the back road of the yard.

Above - No. 33018 with its short train waits in the platform. Because watering facilities at Midhurst had been withdrawn, a tender engine had to be used. The pretty minimal load on this occasion consists of two grain wagons, a 5-plank open and a brake van. Too early as yet for the sugar beet harvest that will swell traffic. Pipes are being unloaded from the four open wagons in the dock road.

Opposite page - Still at Petworth with more detail of the LBSCR signal box and a close up of 33018. The 75E shed plate it carries indicates that it is now based at Three Bridges. By the time this locomotive was withdrawn in July 1965, only five of the original 40 remained in service.

Next page - The same locomotive waits for time. There is no point in leaving early: it would only have had to wait at Hardham Junction. The crew are no doubt enjoying a cup of tea in the station building.

Following page - The view from the road overbridge at the western end of Petworth showing the station and yard with No. 33018 and its train waiting to depart.

Previous Page - On to Selham. Like the previous two stations it was also built of wood. To my mind it was the prettiest of the branch stations, situated on a low embankment in the centre of the tiny village it served. This view was taken in September 1963. As you look east towards Petworth the siding for the cattle dock is visible on the right. The animals reached it by means of a long sloping track from the road.

Opposite top - Selham asleep in the midday sun. The cut straw yellowing in the foreground echoes the fading paintwork.

Opposite bottom - Selham station looking towards Midhurst. The tiny goods yard is beyond the station building on the right. Like Fittleworth the points were unlocked by a key on the train staff.

Above - The end of the line. Midhurst station in October 1963 looking towards Selham. Unlike the other stations on this line this had been a grand affair. It was built to the LBSCR 'Country House' station design, with two platforms and a bay. Sadly by this time dereliction has already set in.

The old stations on the Midhurst line have fared better than most. Fittleworth, after many years of neglect, is now sympathetically restored as a private house. Petworth was granted Grade 2 listed status and survives today as a stylish hotel and restaurant with Pullman cars in the platform. Selham still stands although its status is unclear. Only Midhurst has been obliterated, replaced by a housing estate.

The Isle of Wight system is very special to me, reviving as it does happy childhood memories. A day on the Island meant sun, steam and excitement. I must have visited it a dozen times in the 1960s. Whereas in volume one I focused on the stretch from Ryde to Ventnor, this time I explore the line to Cowes. Although far less busy, with just a basic hourly service, it offered good opportunities for photography. The certainty of seeing these old but beautifully maintained trains, the attractive landscape and the seeming inevitability of bright sunshine made a trip to the Island memorable indeed.

Opposite top - A view of Ryde Pier taken from a train standing at the Pier Head station on Platform 1 with the town of Ryde just visible in the distance. Another train has left Ryde Esplanade and is now travelling along the pier towards us.

Opposite bottom - Standing at the end of the platform at the same station I was struck by the precision of the arrangements required to fit trains into the space available. While on the right the crew of No. W20 'Shanklin' finish taking water, on the left the driver of No. W18 'Ningwood' looks back for a green flag from the guard.

Above - On another occasion, in June 1964, No. W18 'Ningwood' is seen pulling out of Ryde Esplanade station. This locomotive is an example of the 'O2' tank engines designed by William Adams for the LSWR in 1888. A total of 23 of them had been shipped to the Island between May 1923 and April 1949. By 1964 they were some of the oldest locomotives in service in the country.

Next page - No. W27 'Merstone' has left the Esplanade station and is about to enter the narrow Ryde tunnel. During the 50s and 60s the Isle of Wight was a major holiday destination. This photograph shows a wonderful collection of motor coaches waiting to take visitors on a tour around the Island.

Previous page - The signal is set for the Cowes line as No. W14 'Fishbourne' approaches Smallbrook Junction. As in this instance trains to Cowes usually had four coaches. Considerable luggage space was required on these holiday routes and the SECR brake coaches with their greater capacity were habitually run at the north end of the train. This reduced the distance the luggage had to be trolleyed from train to boat. The lower capacity LBSCR brakes were positioned at the south end.

Opposite top left - *No.* W14 'Fishbourne' is waiting at Smallbrook Junction until it can leave the single line. There has been a minor derailment at the Pier Head and this summer Saturday service is having problems. However the delay offers a chance to take a good look at the vintage coaches that form set 486.

Opposite bottom - No. W24 'Calbourne' heads away from Smallbrook Junction with a train for Cowes. The fireman has just collected the single line token. This engine is carrying 'Duty number board' 13. Such boards were carried on summer Saturdays to help the signalmen set the correct route at exceptionally busy times.

Above - The first station on the Cowes line was Ashey. This has always been one of my favourites. The old station building and the platform on the right were in use when I first came here in the mid 1950s. However a new platform and shelter had to be built because of subsidence. These were located on the site of the former siding and can be seen alongside. Ashey once boasted a racecourse on this spot but by the 1960s there was no sign of it.

Previous page - No. W26 'Whitwell' leaves Ashey on a sunny summer afternoon. The old station building is starting to show signs of neglect.

Opposite top - An unidentified 'O2' enters Haven Street with a train from Ryde and the signalman prepares to collect the single line token. This station had a solitary island platform and the station building, seen on the left, was at ground level, not on the platform at all.

Opposite bottom - No. W14 'Fishbourne' departs Haven Street for Ryde, seen off by the signalman who has just handed over the single line token to the crew. It was normal practice for trains to cross here.

Above - There were two stations between Haven Street and Newport: Wootton and Whippingham, both closed by this time. Here Whippingham station is seen from a passing train.

This page - No. W14 'Fishbourne' seen here waiting to leave Newport for Ryde. The brick viaduct, shown opposite, is immediately ahead of the train. The former line to Sandown diverged to the right at the start of the viaduct.

Opposite top - No. W27 'Merstone' is seen waiting in the bay platform at Newport formerly used by branch trains to Freshwater. Curiously these trains had to back out of the bay platform for a short distance before they could change direction and head off down the branch. The extensive locomotive and carriage sheds and the sidings, now largely unused, can be seen beyond the water tower

Opposite bottom - No. W31 'Chale' heads over Newport viaduct towards Ryde. The engine has a replacement Drummond boiler with safety valves on top of the dome. These boilers were reckoned to be inferior to the older Adams ones, less free steaming and more prone to priming. Locomotives with these boilers tended to be allocated to the less onerous workings on the Cowes line rather than the heavy work required of Ventnor trains.

Opposite top - No. W31 'Chale' waits at Mill Hill station on the outskirts of Cowes on the last leg of its journey. This station had just one single platform; there was no goods yard.

Opposite bottom - An ex LSWR 'Road Van', S56046, still painted in Southern Railway brown, seen in the small goods yard at Cowes. The Isle of Wight system had several of these SR, Diagram 154, brake vans together with a few others rebuilt into more exotic forms. The entire Island's freight stock was pretty antique. As it was little used there was no incentive to update it.

Above - A general view of Cowes station with the signal box, sidings and coal yard. Unusually there is a train in the right hand platform. After the closure of the Sandown line this platform was rarely used. Perhaps they are adding an extra coach. The formation does appear to be five vehicles. Maybe it was 'Cowes week'.

Next page - Cowes station in its delightful setting. No. W24 'Calbourne' waits to depart. It alone was to survive and be preserved. The longevity of the O2 class and their ability to haul heavy trains even in old age was a reflection of the excellence of William Adams' design.

The line from Smallbrook Junction to Cowes closed on 21st February 1966. The section from Smallbrook to Whippingham has now been restored and reopened by the Isle of Wight Steam Railway who have their headquarters at Haven Street. Newport has been totally obliterated and Cowes? I haven't been back to see.

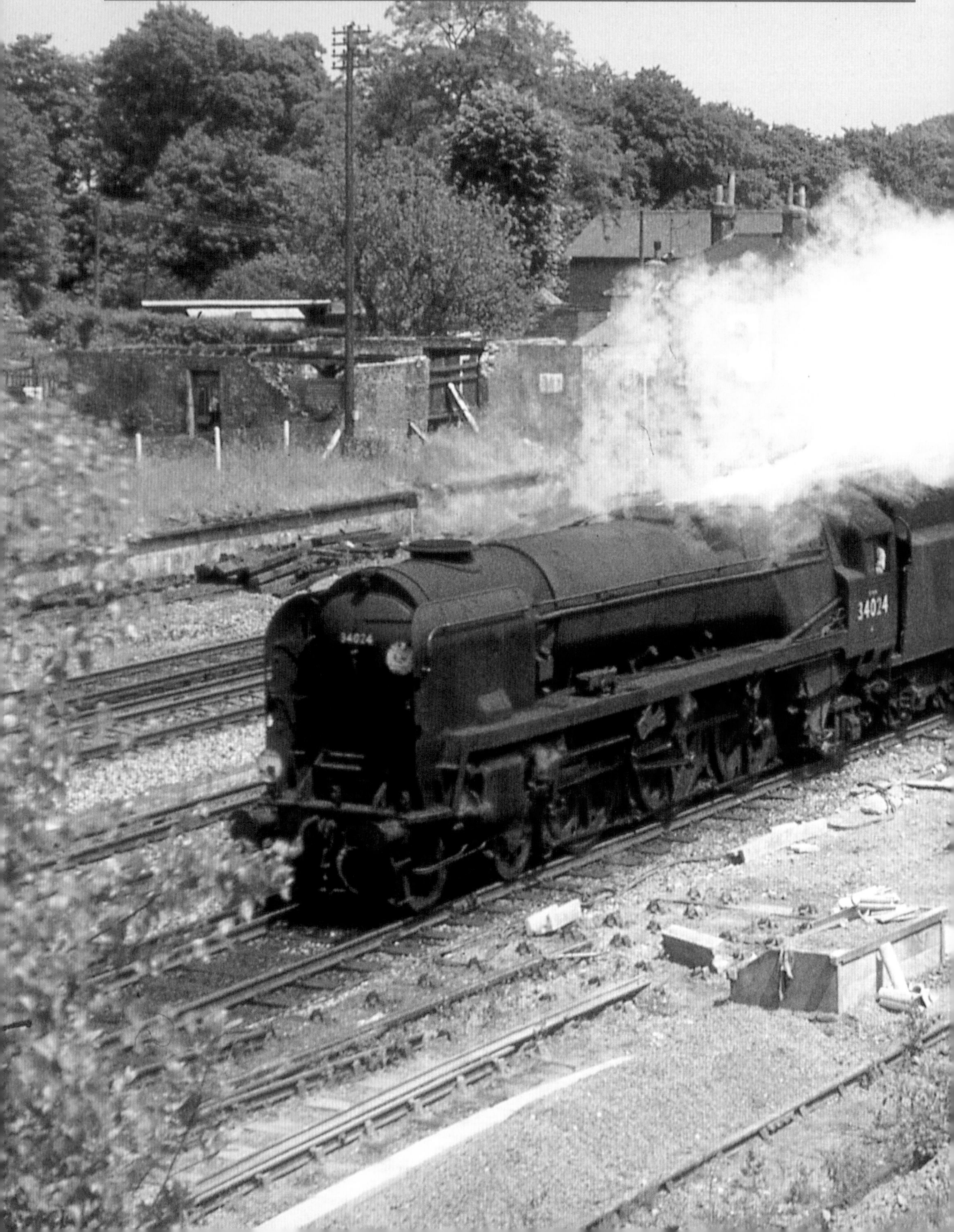
34024
34024

CHAPTER 6

THE SOUTH WESTERN MAIN LINE

By 1967 steam was in terminal decline throughout the country. The neighbouring Western Region had already eliminated it altogether. However, the South Western main line running from Waterloo to Bournemouth and Salisbury still retained it. This was in fact the last steam operated main line in the country but even here all was over by July when steam on the Southern ceased completely. On several previous occasions I had tried to take photographs here but without success. The weather or the light had been wrong and the results disappointing. The breakthrough came in early summer 1967, in the final few weeks of operation, when I was fortunate to get two days in ideal conditions to record some of the last workings.

Previous page - The Pullman train has always been iconic, a symbol of opulence. What luck to find myself in the right place on the right day to capture a shot of the down 'Bournemouth Belle' hauled by steam. Here we see it passing through Winchfield, on the down slow line, behind No. 34024 'Tamar Valley' one of the rebuilt West Country Pacifics.

Above - On the same day in late June 1967 again at Winchfield, No. 34102 'Lapford' an original West Country passes through with a down freight.

Opposite top - The four track section near Winchfield provided good photographic opportunities. Here No. 73085 a British Railways Standard Class 5 heads west with a freight train.

Opposite bottom - The same train seen from above with a load of concrete sleepers in the first few vehicles. These are destined for relaying work further down the line.

Opposite top - Diesel had already replaced steam on some trains as is the case here with a maroon liveried 'Warship' heading a Waterloo - Exeter express passenger service.

Opposite bottom - Some of the Permanent Way trains were also diesel hauled. This empty rail train is being worked by BRCW Type 3 (later class 33) No. D6511.

Above - Rebuilt West Country No. 34100 'Appledore' pulls away from Basingstoke with a train bound for Plymouth. The steam engine will probably only take it as far as Salisbury. In common with most of the survivors by this time, No. 34100 appears without nameplates and with its number just painted on the smokebox.

Next page - A rebuilt Merchant Navy ambles by with a freight destined for Southampton Docks It's hard to see the number but my guess is that it is No. 35028 'Clan Line' The Merchant Navy class was originally designed for mixed traffic but the rebuilds were rarely seen on freight except towards the end of their lives.

Previous page - A few years earlier in August 1963, 28xx 2-8-0 locomotive No. 2856 approaches Worting Junction with a train of sleeper wagons, probably destined for Redbridge depot. The headcode indicates a ballast working. Western Region engines were not uncommon on the SW mainline, in fact WR locomotives ran regular passenger services on a daily basis as well as the occasional freight train and excursion. No. 2856 was based at Oxley and was withdrawn in April 1964.

(author's collection)

Above - Lord Nelson No. 30852 'Sir Walter Raleigh' was withdrawn in February 1962. It is pictured here as it swings into Basingstoke with a down train for Bournemouth. The driver wearing sunglasses and a dirty cap pays careful attention as he draws into the station: the fireman has his tea can at the ready. Perhaps he has arranged to get a fresh brew here.

(author's collection)

Opposite top - At Worting Junction, just west of Basingstoke, the Salisbury / West of England and Bournemouth / Weymouth lines diverged. Here Standard Class 5 4-6-0 No. 73020 heads a Salisbury line train beyond the junction.

Opposite bottom - Heading in the opposite direction is a rebuilt Pacific with a short passenger train.

Next page - Pretty little Oakley station stands closed, its canopy partly demolished, a backdrop to Standard Class 5 No. 73043 as it thunders through with a train for Salisbury.

Opposite top - From the Salisbury direction Standard class 4 tank No. 80133 at the head of a van train passing the ex LSWR signal box. The crew seem to be trying to go as fast as they can. Certainly one of the fastest freight trains I have ever seen, with the box vans swaying and bouncing along like a string of corks.

Opposite bottom - The same train roars past. Then quietness returns. All that remains are the lineside fires left in its wake.

Above - Late June 1967. A general view of Oakley station looking towards Salisbury. The station had closed on 17th June 1963. It was a typical LSWR wayside station with its now closed signalbox, lamp posts and an armless lattice signal post all still in place.

Opposite top - A 3-coach Western Region DMU heads away from Oakley with a stopping train for Basingstoke. The point timbers visible on the right indicate that there used to be access to a siding here.

Opposite bottom - Standard Class 5 No. 73024 heads an up train through Whitchurch in the evening light.

Above - Winchester was one of my favourite places when I first started train spotting. There was a little park above the City station where I used to sit and eat my sandwiches and watch a succession of down trains headed by 'Lord Nelsons' stopping in the platform. Then a walk down through the city to the decaying Chesil station and a 'Great Western' ride back to Eastleigh. No Lord Nelson in this shot of the City station unfortunately. It is a rebuilt Pacific with its maroon BR coaches on an 'inter-regional' that pulls in. At this date the platforms are being extended in preparation for electrification. The water column is in danger of being left high and dry halfway down the platform. In any case it won't be needed much longer.

Opposite top - Shawford station between Winchester and Eastleigh was near the junction for the Didcot, Newbury and Southampton line. There was a down loop avoiding the platforms for the exclusive use of DN&S trains that can be seen on the right. This photograph taken in May 1966 shows ex LMS Black 5 44856 thundering through on the mainline with an excursion train from Coventry.

(author's collection)

Opposite bottom - And so on to Eastleigh, with memories of many happy hours spent watching trains. Eastleigh was a place where I could be sure of seeing my favourite Southern and Great Western engines. The latter came in along the DN&S or the line from Reading to Basingstoke. This latter had regular 'Hall' workings as well as through excursions. This shot of No. 7922 'Salford Hall' entering Eastleigh station with a down excursion train was therefore a must. No. 7922 was withdrawn in December 1965.

(author's collection)

Above - It's June 1967, early evening. An old spotting haunt, Campbell Road, leading to Eastleigh shed and works. Tonight it is deserted. Rebuilt Battle of Britain No. 34090 'Sir Eustace Missenden Southern Railway' has come out of the shed yard with a weed killing train. The engine has lost its nameplates but is still reasonably clean. The fireman is on top of the tender probably clearing a coal blockage in preparation for the work ahead.

Next page - Out comes 'Lapford', No. 34102, an original Pacific, followed by 'Clovelly', No. 34037 a rebuilt Pacific incredibly still carrying its name plates. The two engines pose for a moment in front of the Eastleigh Works Office. They will probably soon be backing down to Southampton Docks to collect boat trains. The crews lean out eagerly waiting for the signal, no doubt relishing the thought on this perfect June evening of one last non-stop dash to Waterloo before it's all over. Still clean, still proud. For me its time to go home. I couldn't face the last day of steam on the Southern, not after this.